A Place to Fall Into

A Place to Fall Into

Jo-Ann Birch

POEMS

Self-published by Jo-Ann Birch
P.O. Box 2146
Santa Cruz, CA 95063

Printed by CreateSpace, a DBA of On-Demand Publishing, LLC.

ISBN 978-1453886557

Library of Congress Catalog Card Number:
2010918610

ACKNOWLEDGMENTS

These poems all were inspired from a space created by Amber Coverdale Sumrall. For their support and good work, I thank Amber and members of the Thursday night writing group: Kim Scheiblauer, Ziggy Rendler-Brenman, Gail Brenner, Julie Hannah Brower, Vicki Nunez and Jessica Woods.

Thanks to *In Celebration of the Muse* presented by Amber Coverdale Sumrall and Dena Taylor, and *Poet/Speak* presented by Len Anderson for inviting me to read at their events.

Thanks also to Sharon Swenson, Darcy Thole, Fran Gertler, Samatha Bartells, Kim Tyler, Johna Tolch and Rosie Christian for their love and laughter.

Nothing becomes real until my wife, Kath, hears the words I've written.

CONTENTS

THEN

SOONER

NOW

for
Boo

A Place to Fall Into

The ocean refuses no river.
Lila Flood

I
tried painting,
but it was easier to fly slicing
potatoes.
Rabia

THEN

Family Bible

At thirteen I found the bible,
top shelf, between my sister's wedding album
and my father's accordion folder
marked *Important Papers.*

Still smelling new after two decades,
its maroon leather cover sported
a picture of Jesus with some sheep,
and a satin bookmark parked in *Genesis.*

Whisper thin pages
edged in gold,
so when shut,
it resembled a brick of goodness.

The words of Jesus in red,
in case of confusion,
colored illustrations sprinkled throughout,
everyone looking perpetually worried.

Near the back, my mother had neatly written
statistics on each of her children.
God only allowed enough space for four,
so she listed me under *Things to Remember.*

Moving Day

In the summer of 1964, my mother carries me on her hip from the small landing at the kitchen door, down the three steps to our driveway. Here we go again, moving for the fourth time, and I am only three. *Win, I'm putting Jo-Ann in the back of the van. Righteeo.* My sister, Elizabeth, and I jump on the stacked mattresses for the block and a half ride to our new PMQ duplex. Tumbling from side to side, we push off each other, falling onto the boxy beds. We explore our new house together: clean hardwood floors, views of pine trees and berry ridden fields, a cement walled basement for my orange rubber ball. After calling dibs on where our beds will be in our new room, we spend the afternoon flying into boxes piled at the foot of the front porch, as our parents arrange the furniture of yet another new start.

From

I am from Camp Borden, the birthplace of the Royal Canadian Air Force. From a pilot and his war bride,

and woods and fields that go forever north.

I am from Canadian Club and Molson Golden, from Sandeman Sherry brawls that kept us all awake at night,

from being told my fingers and toes would fall off if they got too cold, and that tapeworms lived inside people's bodies, possibly mine.

I am from falling in love with Vicky, who knew how to hug and kiss my brother Bobby, then disappeared after nine months,

from never having to go to church, my father answering the door *Jesus Christ, who is it?* if he suspected Jehovah's Witness.

I am from rows of purple lilacs in bloom, their honeyed scent marking the end of the school year,

and warm summer nights, roasting marshmallows on sticks carved to perfect points by my father, and jumping off the high dive at Outlet River, lifted on a rush of green water,

from my brother Michael torturing us as he recited the song *Bingo* over and over from the backseat,

and Winnipeg Beach where my sister Elizabeth begged and cried to get a hotdog, only to have a horsefly land in it.

I am from the sophisticated turning of leaves in October, a place to fall into at full speed,

from Yorkshire pudding, roast beef gravy, and buttery sausage rolls for Christmas dinner.

I am from the vacuum cleaner finding its way into every holiday photograph, from white ice skates, house-high snowdrifts, and a block heater to keep the car engine from freezing at night.

I am from a worn pathway in the olive green carpet as my sister Lois practiced her model walk, volume K-L of the encyclopedia balanced on her head,

from a sense of humor, sharp as a diver's knife, slicing the thick kelp cords that tried to hold us all in place.

I am from searching through overflowing ashtrays on Sunday mornings for lipsticked cigarette butts, from men with missing teeth and women with bare asses asleep on our living room carpet.

I am from a giggling commitment that *God Save the Queen* each morning, and straight *A* high schools neither parent had to visit.

I am from Elizabeth leaving home before my fourteenth birthday and my odyssey to catch up with her someday in another country.

Now I am from that country.

Being a Girl

I love to watch girls spend time being girls
because it had never occurred to me.

The Queen

I knew she'd regret it,
but Amanda didn't want to go.

So Lizzy and I walked the three miles
along Saskatchewan Avenue,
between the scrawny treed suburb
and the yellow wheat fields.

The train was stopped
at the place where a nameless
road crossed the track.
We ran the last length
of the Pullmans to the small
crowd who'd heard about her visit
on their AM car radios.

She was climbing into a cream
colored carriage, four white horses,
Princess Anne and Prince Charles
already perched on maroon seats.
I poked my bad haircut
through the crowd of stiffening smiles,
covered the stains of my shirt.

She waved to us as her carriage
crossed the tracks, towards the city.
I slid my dirty feet below
my bum, rocking side to side,
but her stare never really
met the crowd, flying
instead just above it.

Lizzy and I walked home,
how could Amanda have missed it?

We were 8 & 10 and we'd been to see the Queen.

Audrey's Cottage

Audrey's second husband was wealthy. They owned a split-level house with pool on the outskirts of Toronto, a six-bedroom cottage on Georgian Bay with boat and dock. This filled my mother and I with wanting, made my father grow more quiet. They invited us up for a weekend in July. The teenage boys taught me how to water-ski in my new Speedo one-piece. *Strong arms. Follow the wake. Pretty good for a girl.* Several cocktails into Saturday afternoon, my mother announced she wanted to try too. After a brief lesson in safety, she haphazardly donned the life belt and tried over and over to get up on the skis. Her failed attempts ate up the better part of dusk, too late for me to have another turn. Audrey made something unrecognizable in a bowl for dinner. Her daughter, Brenda, and I were the youngest, so we had to eat first. My father leaned against the stove, cigarette smoke encircling the rye whisky in his hand while the others talked of Trudeau. I waited for Brenda to look away, then scooped my dinner into her bowl causing my father to howl with laughter. Before dinner, he had shown her how he could make me flinch just by touching his belt buckle. On the drive home, I watched the road for three full hours, as if by my own will I could keep the car safe.

A Way Beyond

Because we didn't have the money for a horse,
my sister saddled up the front hall banister.
Pillow for a saddle, yellow karate belt for reins,
she worked on it for weeks.

Adding more and more gear for her trek:
my brother's green canteen on the left,
a rolled up blue towel behind,
her hat over the banister ball.

Each day after school she sat high on her horse,
tipping her hat up and down,
slapping the reins from side to side,
as she made clip clop sounds,
tongue to teeth, endlessly.

She was afforded this fantasy,
undisturbed, for three months,
(no one had a need for any of the gear).
The banister stayed saddled,
as she rode in solitude every evening.

It was the happiest I can remember her,
planning her escape.

Avoiding the Morning Chore

Why bother? I am only going to get in it again tonight.

It will take too long.

I like it that way.

I can't disturb the cat, she's sleeping.

And her kittens.

I must leave to get to school on time.

Yes, but it's my mess.

The sheets want to see the sunlight.

Can I get an allowance if I do?

It matches my closet now.

Elizabeth never does.

But I'm only going to mess it up again later.

Three Weekends on Lake Scugog

In the winter, when I was 21,
the temperature dropped
below zero for weeks
without snow.

Lake Scugog became
a solid sheet of ice,
one foot thick,
miles long and wide.

My brothers and I
brought blankets,
our ice skates
and sailed all Sunday.

The next weekend
they shot a hockey puck,
careful not to miss or
chance skating forever to fetch it.

Way out past them
I noticed the ice beneath me
was dark black,
I wondered why.

I skated back to my brother's
white ice and listened
to the cracking sounds
ricocheting across the lake.

It snowed all week
so when we returned
we brought shovels
for a hockey rink.

Later, a snowmobiler watched
his machine sink to the bottom
at the same dark spot
I had stood the weekend before.

Moving to Manitoba

The train rocked like a heartbeat,
ties and gravel exposed, accordion connectors,
as I navigated from car to car.
Diners smiled at my conversation, full-bellied joy.
So far, this was the best part of moving.

Sharing a berth with my sisters and mother, pale
green walls, corduroy couches, window half-way down.
With a rhythm of rails to mark our journey,
the Frasier River fell far behind,
our new city miles ahead lit up the prairie sky.

My father reported that the neighbor boy, Kevin,
kept ringing the doorbell to see if I'd moved in yet.
The leaves on Campbell Street were turning
as we unpacked our seasoned suitcases,
just in time for first grade.

Double Knit

My father bought a pair of pants in the 70s – double knit polyester, orange and brown plaid. They hung on him like a limp dishrag, sagging at the knees and bum. He wore them because we hated them, gleeful at our disgust. One evening he fell asleep watching TV with a lit cigarette, which burned a canoe shaped hole in the right leg. He took it upon himself to repair the pants, cutting a piece of the hem and sewing it into place. *No one will notice that*, he told my mother. *Not as long as you're moving at a full gallop*, she replied. After that, she didn't let him shop alone.

Birth

My mother told the story so often, I knew it by heart. *When I found out I was pregnant with Jo-Ann, I thought,* 'Win is going to kill me… one more mouth to feed.' *So, I got a bucket and began to scrub the walls and ceilings. The next week I went to the doctor and he said,* "Mrs. Birch, you are on a verge of having a massive miscarriage," *he reached in with two fingers and tilted my uterus back. Some months later Jo-Ann was born – downy soft hair, big brown eyes and perfectly poised hands like this – such a beautiful baby.* When I reached my thirties I asked her to stop telling the story. *Oh,* she said and never mentioned it again.

Northerly Neighbor

I am from Canada

where nothing much happened,

and if it did,

we were too drunk to notice.

Unlike the States,

where each week

the country toiled

over some new drama.

We just laughed,

and lit another cigarette,

"I think it's your deal."

Questions from a Three Year Old

are you going to die?
what happened to the cat who got caught in the dryer?
where is she now?
can we get a cat?
I had a bad dream, can I sleep in your bed?
will the ocean cause a flood?
do I *have* to eat this?
how did shells get here?
how high is the sky?
can we get a cat?
can we go the beach again tomorrow?
can I sleep with you?
are you going to die?

Tenth Birthday

We had just moved to another new town,
too soon to have any friends.
It was a Thursday night, my father
took me with him grocery shopping.
The snow had started.

He pushed the cart through the aisles.
Indicating the row with games and toys,
Go pick a game for your birthday.
The fluorescent lights bounced
back from the dark, wide windows.

Scanning the titles,
I grabbed a *Spirograph* game,
and ran to catch up with my father,
who hurried through his list so we could
get to the Liquor Store before it closed.

To Believe

It wasn't so much that
I thought Santa would
come down the chimney,

as it was that he made
my parents behave,
if only for one day.

One Thing My Mother Explains

At twelve, Elizabeth asked my mother about sex. Being a practical woman, she thought it best to kill two birds with one stone and so included me in the explanation. I was eight. My mother called us into her bedroom. Propped up against the pillows, with Elizabeth on one side and I on the other, she began, "The penis of the man goes into the vagina of the woman, then the sperm fertilizes the egg." Silence. She was clearly in over her head. Elizabeth looked horrified as my mother explained the procedure several times, as if by repetition we would understand. Finally I broke the cycle and asked, "How does the semen get out, does the man pee in her or something?" My mother laughed, "No, no," but she wouldn't say how. She just smiled, not knowing how to continue. After a very long pause Elizabeth and I both grew up to be lesbians.

Acrostic Childhood

Call me home
Head of stone
Ivy wrapped nest
Life's final test
Death comes sweet
Heaven complete
Over the wall
Old woman calls
Day is done, come home

SOONER

Becoming Unstuck

Like a horse struggling to free itself
from a muddy creek,
my sister writhes and blames,
only to sink deeper.
I stand on the creek side,
having just escaped,
still scraping mud off,
inches from the edge.

Was it Jesus who said, "Touch me not,
for I am not yet ascended?"
So fresh, this new freedom.
I am this close to joining her.
We would laugh, ignore the mud,
the lack of air and imminent death.
Yet I would have her company, if only for a while.

She won't take my advice, and rightly so,
advice only thickens the mud.
An outstretched hand cannot close the chasm,
she must make her own way.
I wait on the side,
risk her drowning or dying of exhaustion,
and do nothing but envision her freedom.

Pray for us both.
Pray for our healing, we two.
As I watch, my sister turns her face
to catch the setting sun.

Brass Spoon

She gave me the spoon, I think in anticipation of her own death,
although it was my father who was dying,
but who can keep track of such details under grief's heel?

I had admired the spoon in passing as a teenager,
and so it became mine.

She talked of how there were only three of these spoons made,
that her aunt gave one to each of her
cousins, and the third came to her.
"My sister always wanted that spoon," she quipped,
wiping her chin with the back of her hand.

Here it sits now on a shelf in my living room,
hardly noticed since being unpacked from the move years ago.
With each visit she holds it and remarks that I should shine it up.

This is how she spends her time, over knick knacks:
Wedgwood and Tiffany and Irish crystal,
on glass shelves, waiting dutifully to be admired.

Handed Down

When I asked my father as a teenager how to parent, he replied,
Hold tight with loose hands, gripping and loosening his neat, able
hands in demonstration. My son has two mothers, and so to be fair
I have become a father of sorts. I coax him out to see the stuff of
the world, train trips, camping, museums. Yesterday, as I watched
him ski from side to side down the gleaming mountain snow,
following him, leaving room for his own wide turns, I understood
what my father meant.

Beyond

Single candlelight,
like a tear in the story
to the other side.

The Adoption

In the mint green hospital room, I notice every gesture of your
birth family. The lilting voices, how often they pass you around,
the unanswered questions when our eyes meet. The self-assured

grandfather, with your same smile, has made an exception
to come together again, for his daughter's sake. The grandmother
has talked herself into this moment, on the edge

of relenting, always one hand on her daughter.
The aunt, fixing her hair, doesn't notice how the angels
have placed a finger on your lips, indenting them

in sleepy silence. And the mother, so young,
has gathered teenage friends, tattooed and smelly,
their nervous giggles prop up her courage. We sit

at the foot of her bed, smile at our good fortune.
Some grand entitlement reserved for royalty and the well
to do. In near disbelief we lay claim to this moment,

taking what has been promised us. I insist on giving you
your first bottle and in that small initiation, your new
breath on my hand, I am without a doubt that we and you

were meant to be. Through the odds of biology and chance
connections, through the web of satellites you had to maneuver
to land on earth, through convincing my wife to consider

adoption, you have fallen into my arms, this perfect
baby boy. We carry you away in borrowed blue flannel,
away from this brief connection of origin, knowing

that as enormous as our gratitude will always be, so too
will be your grief. And we quietly accept all of this
driving home on that icy, April afternoon.

September 11th

I looked down from the window,
blown out by the explosion,
and had to decide whether to burn or fly.

I opened my arms and decided to fly.

Choir Practice: *for Kath*

I had lost my way.
She said sing from your heart.

Does she know
that I cannot hear the beat
through the boards of wood,
and stones and bricks
that I have spent a lifetime constructing,
placing between each wound, each sorrow?

Now with every prayer,
every connection
to a source more powerful
there is cause to remove a weathered piece:

a blue board
that I had placed at four years old
when I arrived home and found no one,
was removed on a Tuesday last year.

In January, I pulled away a red brick
added in tenth grade
when a teacher read my work out loud
only to claim it incoherent,

and a large granite rock tumbled aside
when I first held my baby son.
I can't recall how it got there.

She asks me to sing from my heart,
but I can just now hear the beat
through thinning layers of boards and stones
as I clear away my fort of protection,
brick by brick.

And it is the singing that brings the prayers
and the healing, inviting each note to land
on this soft, strong vessel
that is my heart.

Closing the Cabin

She was in transition to becoming a *he.*
Thick brown crop, baggy shorts,
droopy, grey tank top.
The hair grew on his legs and armpits.
His voice still high, no Adam's Apple yet,
I avoided looking at his crotch,
unsure of what to look for.

Our hosts, a longtime lesbian couple,
gave him first dibs on the manly chores,
there was no one over six years old
with an XY combination.
He tackled each task with furrowed brow,
looking satisfied, seen.

I held back, as I always had
in road hockey, touch football, kick the can
when the red-faced boys,
bruised and sweaty,
would stare me down, call me *a guy.*

But, when the chainsaw
found its way into his hands,
threatening us and the cabin,
I pushed the red-faced voices aside
and asked, *Mind if I give you a hand?,*
made the necessary cuts,
and felled the tree in a safe direction.

For the rest of the weekend
our hosts chirped again and again,
You sure are handy with a chainsaw.

Little did they know.

The Reality of Doing

He said the stage is like a high wire performance.
He said actors need to understand the stakes before
they climb up there.
He said just move from moment to unanticipated moment,
don't think.
He said his children were more important than New York.
He said he loved New York.
He said he would have preferred to be a dancer.
He said I was a good listener.

Sometimes I'd love to work with him again.
Sometimes I miss him more than I ever thought.
Sometimes I imagine what he'd say.
Sometimes I wish I knew what I'd had.

Three Springs

They were made in the northeast by
iron workers pouring orange liquid into form.
A powerful little machine then coiled
the steel into clever spring shapes.
Now standing, dutiful bookends,
holding up my garage door.

Another bite, this time on my left wrist.
I hold my cat under the warm water,
lather up his back and neck.
He howls, legs clenched.
The skin shines white between his toes,
as fleas spring from his wet fur.

With the melting snow, and longer days,
all life awakens, including the biting bugs.
Grateful for the sun to dry my cat,
who's already forgiven me,
I welcome spring, dry my hands,
and close the garage door.

Brigid and John

Three months after his wife's death,
John had their two dogs put down,
paid and posted the utility bill,
and walked into Lake Ontario.

Of all my mother's friends,
they were the most gentle.
Laughing on our sectional couch, always
Brigid sat straight, John leaned towards her.

He left the keys in the ignition,
a note to their children on the dashboard.
Apart from feeling shattered,
I couldn't help but admire his sense of order.

Like the symmetry of sago pondweed,
wavelike in the Great Lake.

People I Notice

Robert De Niro can't tell a lie.
Jodi Foster is brilliant, but hides her passion.
Tom Cruise never lets us forget how hard he's working.
Bette Davis was fantastic.
Jack Lemon understood the craft.
Sigourney Weaver is funnier than she thinks.
Cate Blanchett is a beautiful chameleon.
Owen Wilson is my comic hero,
Ellen DeGeneres, my gay hero.
It's not clear if Al Pacino even likes his profession.
Kate Winslet is good enough to laugh at fame.
Madonna is all about love.
Ingrid Bergman held the light.
Robert Redford's heart is in the right place.
Meryl Streep gives white people a good name.
Judi Dench hardly has to say a word.
Mr. Eastwood, *way to go man!*

Saturday Afternoon

She had to attend another *Inner Light* conference,
something about struggling to find paradise.

We worked all afternoon to surprise her:
redwood sides, chicken wire bottom, ten bags of soil.

His small hands carefully placed each lettuce plant,
keeping the sun off the pale roots.

The tomatoes and basil could be buried in their pots.
What will they think of next?

As I watered the speckled dirt, he remembered the carrot
seeds on his shelf, a gift from his pre-school teacher.

When she got home we covered her eyes, led her outside,
and her smile completed our paradise.

Edge of Play

Dressed in his batman costume, a pirate patch,
and cowboy hat, he kept an eye out
as his buddy weaved a Spiderman web
of blankets across the top bunk.
Five year old deities,
their puffy muscles taking on the world.

I clung to the door jam, pressed against the wall.
Noticing me, he looked down.
I inched away, *Don't go Mama.*

As I moved into his room, all action stopped.
I called them by their superhero names.
He tore off the eye patch,
Mama, I told you. Only call me by my real name.
Having shattered his make-believe world,
I retreated to the kitchen.

Then looking for them when dinner was done,
I passed the crumpled costumes in the hall.

Springtime Vacation

I stand beside my mother
in the vineyard outside of Venice.
She hangs on every word
the winemaker says,
like gospel from Jesus,
a secret recipe for inebriation.
I don't drink.

But wander away,
render myself invisible,
to the garden's sweet calm.
Brushing against the pink of lilies,
I watch the bees at noon
gather bits of yellow dust
to feed the day.

How we cling to each other
long past what is necessary.
As my mother samples the many wines,
I gather the lilies closer
and envy the bees
as they fly away,
far away into April.

Latter Day Saints of Eldorado

there are no laugh lines around their eyes
these women lined up at the Texas compound
trapped in a web of secrets and lies
murmurs of *my sweet* the only sound

these women line up at the Texas compound
whose children believe devils dwell in water
murmurs of *my sweet* the only sound
as foster parents pine for sons and daughters

children who believe devils dwell in water
fear everyone outside - child, woman and man
while foster parents pine for sons and daughters
and contemplate crayons in unpracticed hands

they fear everyone outside - child, woman and man
one child questioned cannot count her siblings
or contemplate crayons in unpracticed hands
the one with twelve wives has long left the building

one child questioned cannot count her siblings
trapped in a web of secrets and lies
the one with twelve wives has long left the building
there are no laugh lines around their eyes

To Live in the Mercy of God

outside my window I see
oak trees, grape vines, daisies

our morning prayers wrap around us
like these cream-colored sheets

our son's joy is bright, fresh
from a night with his angels

the bathroom tiles shine white
the dog, oh the yellow dog

and this all before breakfast

How to Be an Elderly Lady: *for my mother*

Live in a quiet suburb where your neighbors are
oh-so predictable. Spend your pension wisely:
groceries, vacations, cigarettes.
Learn to play bridge,
know who you have to beat to stay on top.

Work on your fourth degree at the local university.
Take one course a year, read the assigned books,
anguish and stammer over each essay. Notice how
the professors are always younger than you.
Curse those who give you anything less than A's.
Invite everyone you know to your graduation.

Go to the theatre – Stratford in the spring for Shakespeare,
Toronto in the winter for *Wicked*.
Limit your exposure to media, but do watch
Turner Classic Movie Channel.
Read everything you can get your hands on,
except Romance and Westerns.

Visit your children scattered across North America,
keep a tight lip about how they live their lives.
Take the tired mothers to the movies.
Pay for a dinner or two,
offer witty stories over cocktails.

Go to every party you are invited,
wear a snappy new hat and coat.
Entertain guests to show off
your pink living room walls.
Dazzle them with your latest concoction,
Chicken Kiev on Wedgwood china.

Get a Shiatsu, black and white. Give her a French name,
buy her stylish jackets for her daily walks.
Pay no attention to your glaring daughter
as you call, *Bijou, come along my little darling*,
in a tone she thought was reserved exclusively for her.

Making Sense Ghazal

Holding close the secrets of the land,
the farmers keep to their wooden houses and barns.

At the store, where I bought this pen,
they put out a long roll of paper to help us find the right fit.

I sent my mother a poem,
she rewrote it and sent it back.

I deal with alcoholics at family visits,
with the increasing discipline of a rock climber.

Young boys are learning to fire weapons in the Middle East,
my son is learning to color within the lines.

Like the cycle of water, universal laws are at work,
correcting the flow, letting go of every detail.

The People Who Live in my Body

There is a critic, who sounds like my father:
hopeless, doubting, and at times, downright cruel,
who strives for mediocrity,
finds comfort in my failure and wouldn't mind a drink.

There is a child, who knows about fun,
knows its worth and the necessity for play.
She will dance in the living room for the cats,
gauge their reaction, fold over with laughter.
This child understands joy and can't get enough.

There is an accountant, checking items off,
balancing the books, keeping order to everything:
food lists, bills, library books due dates, the best mortgage rate.
She is always counting and I count on her.
This one is highly esteemed, but humble enough
to enjoy the gratification of things being just tickety boo.

There is a mother,
watching with perfect distance.
Who lives in between words and thoughts,
safely nestled, ready to catch a fall, deter a stranger,
or offer something just before the blood sugar drops.
She feels for all living things, heart pounding on her sleeve.

There is a rock star, who knows the moves, the words,
and the way to stand. She plays a mean air guitar
with curled lip, a rageful teenager making art out of fury.
Cool, strong and smart, she wants to be your sledgehammer.

And there is wisdom, a patient, old man,
probably Tibetan,
who watches us all and giggles with glee.

Never Stuck

The night before I left home,
I packed my bags alone in my room
while my parents got drunk in the kitchen.

I checked my passport, plane ticket
and the thousand dollars I'd saved,
tucked away in my leather purse.

I was deciding which coat to bring,
when I heard my parents,
That bitch is finally moving out.
I can't wait for the little cunt to leave.

That was.

Then at church this Sunday,
Kincha, a handsome, tall black woman,
prayed for us saying,
We are here because we are beloved,
we are here because we are wonderful.

Now, who am I to believe?

NOW

Lesbian Mom Hiking With Her Eight Year-Old Son

Hiking can be meditative; trick is
finding a pace and following it.
I'm not sure he hears me.

Passing granite outcrops,
we scramble over a fallen pine.
Mom, this is gonna mess with your pace,

and he stops to pee against a tree.
Echo Lake on our right, solid blue silence.
Pretty handy that you can pee like that.

I just love having a penis, he boasts.
More trees pass, rocks mark the way across a steam.
If you had a penis, I'd let you be...

Not quite hearing him I ask,
If I had a penis, you'd let me be your Dad?
No, if you had a penis I'd let you be in my band.

Oh well, that's even better.

Marriage Bed

Here we go again, another November.
My marriage bed brought out into the streets.
Studied for fatal flaws.
Suspected of social unrest.
A springboard from which to bounce their politics.
A cowardly attempt is made to define the standards
of what it is to be human,
as they pull at the bed covers, poke into the night stand,
trying to expose the root of our deviance.
They are disappointed to find
my marriage bed is as plain and ordinary as all others.
Clean and flat, soundly square,
almost unremarkable.
I always have had one wife.
My marriage bed holds decades of dreams,
sturdy commitment for support.
The stains of resentment are washed each week,
fading and returning as we continue the work
of keeping our love fresh.
A sacred promise of honor weaves through
the dailyness of our lives,
providing warm comfort each night.

I stand by my marriage,
and hope that all we have in common,
carries us through another November.

On This Night

Who can I find to scream and dance with me?

My neighbor's window flickers TV blue green.
My mother is sleeping in a different time zone.
My wife is shopping for underwear at the mall.
My sisters will say, *Uh huh...*
My friends will wonder if he is too far ahead or behind their own
children.

I punch the air in silent jubilation.
Tonight my son has read me *Go, Dog. Go!*
in its entirety.

God's Vocabulary

She speaks in the affirmative,
Yes and *I will.*
Like a doting grandparent,
If that's what you want dear.

Then the laws of the universe
snap at me with consequences,
another painful free-choice lesson.

She just smiles,
tells me *she loves me*
and means it.
Are you ready to try again?
I am,
and head straight into a
self-centered parade of indulgence.

Yes, I will
followed by the sting of karma.
She doesn't make the rules,
only loves me, wants
to give me everything
so I can be happy and free.

She won't give advice.
I must find my own way,
while she supplies
everything I can possibly imagine.

And she repeats,
Anything you want dear,
I am here for you.

It's so annoying.

Gull at Tide Line

It was the dog who found her first
struggling at the edge of the surf.
A thirtyish man approached while
his infant-strapped wife kept her distance.
My sister, visiting from DC, came in next
and with his support, lifted the left wing
to see the fishing line wrapped around her,
the lure tangling her feet.

I ran and asked a group by the rocks,
Do any of you have a knife?
There is a bird caught in some line.
A handy woman and her friend
went to work, cracking the lure in half,
cutting line here, cutting there.

She was too tired to fight.
Five of us huddled close,
no words, clear on our task
to free the gull.
Stepping back we watched
as she tried her wings,
steadied her sea legs,
pushed herself past waves to open water.

The man pocketed the hook,
and caught up with his wife.
The handy woman strolled
with her friend back to their picnic.
My sister stood, staring out to sea.
And I watched as she and the gull
drifted further and further out of reach.

A Hug from Amma

They pushed us into her arms,
those devotees, hearty and precise.
Pulling me to her shoulder
stained with tears and makeup,
her mouth at my ear, she rocked me
ever
so
closely
repeating one word,
"Ma Ma Ma
Ma Ma Ma."

A place to land in the chaos,
recognizing it for the thousandth time.
Infinite motherhood spilled over me,
from somewhere just beyond her.
Divine embrace,
warm
full
joy
flowed through me to my young son,
who had been crying the instant before
they pushed us into her arms.

Tahoe

Blue like no other,
this lake, nearly bottomless.
Boy in a kayak
joyously paddles over
seven hundred years of rain.

Scourge of the Garden

Next year, I will know better
than to invite you into my garden.
Oh sure, you're showy:
jagged macho leaves,
prickly stocks that won't quit,
your phallic fruit reproducing like rabbits,
but, you have taken over.

The pole beans have shrunk and withered,
perhaps from penis envy.
The strawberries are too timid
to show their tender flowers,
for fear you will notice,
throw your stocky self upon them.

The tomato plants are your only competition.
I see how you have intimidated
the one closest to you,
her sister has to reach over
with pep talk vines,
coaxing her onward and upward.

Well, my money is on those two.
They will still be standing,
heavy with fruit, full and sweet,
while you will have long since shot your wad.

Borrowed Lines

Acting stands you up,
brings you to your feet.

You wear her dresses and shade of lipstick,
cut your hair to fit her style,
sit with a straight back.

She makes her way
into the seams of your life,
informing your moods,
until at last,
you become her habits.

Then the lights come up and
a crowd of strangers flies over your life.

(Line borrowed from Naomi Shihab Nye.)

Traveling Along

In the busy airport, I track my son's every move. He and the woman with kind brown eyes strike up a conversation about *Hot Wheels*. He explains the features of *Monster Mutt* and *King Krunch*, demonstrating the wriggly movement of the wheels and how fast they speed across the wide steel window ledge. She smiles broadly, expands her questioning. I share her pride in him, inch closer to their warmth. She hears about his school, the blue bike he got for his seventh birthday, our dog whose name is Zimo, and that his friend Bode has this very same Ferrari, but his is red. Often the most I get when I ask about his day is "good." And I must never hold this against him.

How to Cook Chili

Begin by dicing 1 medium yellow onion.
If you begin to cry, make it about something recent.
In a large pot, melt 1/4 lb. of butter over medium heat,
add onions, sauté until clear.
Add 1 lb. of ground beef, high quality and organic,
thank the cow now grazing in God's garden.
With a wooden spoon, dice meat until brown,
mix with onions.
Put Flamenco music on the stereo,
add some lively steps between the counter and the stove.
Open a large can of tomatoes, a small can of tomato paste,
mix with meat and onions, stirring slowly.
Turn down heat.
Rinse fresh mushrooms,
pick off dirt from the local farm,
slice lengthwise.
Dice a large green pepper.
Turn music up, toss in handfuls of pepper and mushrooms
on each downbeat.
Open 2 cans of kidney beans,
pour into pot while singing loudly words you can make out.
Open a window to cool your steamy self down.
Locate the silver measuring spoon set.
Dance wildly across the kitchen.
Add 2 tablespoons of chili powder.
Lower heat and music, cover pot to simmer.
Leave the house, allowing ingredients the privacy to co-mingle.
Come back in 3 hours, turn off stove and let cool.
Refrigerate for 2 days.
Reheat slowly,
eat with warm black bread and someone you love.

1,949 Delegates:
the day Obama won the nomination

My family vacationed in Washington, DC. On the third day I turned to my sister in-law and asked, *Have you noticed that every single service person, from waiter, to store clerk, to toll booth worker - I mean every single service person we have encountered is a person of color?* She looked me squarely in the face, pink and content, and said, *Really, I hadn't noticed.* And I thought to myself, therein lies the problem.

Mother's Lament

I wish my nights were filled with nothing,
ache for long stretches of nothing in my day.

There is too much of everything: lists of things to do,
people to pay attention to, worries, accolades, connections.

At night my angels put me through fussy, dream-filled lessons.
Everything, it seems, wants something from me.

The alarm rings, which I resent, setting my mind into a race
that goes on throughout the day and most of the night.

Can you walk the dog? Send us a proposal by end of day tomorrow.
I think it's your turn to go to the school assembly. Watch, Mom!

How I long for wide, open fields of limitlessness.
Let me be drenched in boredom, surrounded by emptiness.

Perhaps then I would fall into peaceful solace,
slumber deeply, want for nothing.

Since I Found God

I approach the intersection,
observe the few cars stopped
at their respective corners
and decide to go.

The pinchy crossing guard
blows her whistle, glares at me
as if I've just committed murder.

Forcing a nod in her direction,
I notice the boy she guides
across the street isn't worried,
doesn't even look at me.

As they pass,
I inch forward.
She doubles back,
holds me in her stare
waving the stop sign
for all the slowing cars to see.

If I had not found God,
I would roll down my window,
What's your fucking problem lady?
I would park my car,
double back to her corner
and hit her with that sign.

But, instead I force my breath
in and out
as she yells, *You don't have a brain in your head.*

A police officer smirks as I pass.
From a sea of rage,
I thank God
for saving me
from a ticket
or worse.

The One Who Got Away

We don't want to leave, lingering beside my car,
sidewalk shops way out of my league.
She has the time now that she's retired,
and I can skip work since I own the company,
but we have gone over the respectable limit for lunch.

Even at 50, the waiters swoon over her,
bringing her bread samples, topping her glass endlessly,
touching her shoulder, her arm.
Occasionally they throw me a bone,
some sideways comment,
like a father would to his daughter's fat little friend.

After lunch, I keep the conversation moving as we walk:
my son's piano lessons, how I loathe to exercise,
my menopausal mood swings.
Anything to draw attention away
from the fact that we are alone.

The 80s brought stolen, exquisite kisses
in fancy restaurant bathrooms,
finding the curve of her hips over
Black Russians in San Francisco gay bars,
her whispering, *Be still my heart,*
late on my doorstep.

She had been married to someone she didn't love.
I think I never made enough money for her.

Now we meet for lunch,
count the years I have been
with my partner, she with her new husband.
Between bites of crab and Brie,
we share book titles and our hopes
for Obama, higher education, bio-fuel.

We finish what's on each other's plate,
and watch the world burning up without us.

Facing the Music

She doesn't look her age
in wigs, false teeth, painted nails
and only admits to it when announcing,
Look what I can do at 82.
She just received her fourth university degree.

But now, breathless and furious,
she can't keep up on walks
at the annual family retreat.
And last Monday she admitted,
I just can't fly anymore,
it's so far from what it used to be.

We live in different countries.
A tragedy of distance, and the need for it.
I can't sit with her,
take her to lunch, a movie,
help with laundry, shopping, meals.

I have a son who needs me
to tuck him in at 8 PM and 2 AM,
change his underwear after he has peed.
I have a mortgage, a wife whose own mother
is dying, I have a yellow dog.
Things that wouldn't occur to her.

There is love here in my home,
and with her, it's never clear.
Like a child with a loaded gun,
she is dangerous, needy
and can turn
just
like
that.

But, how will I feel when she's gone?

From: Elizabeth Birch [ebirch@email.com]
Sent: Monday, September 21, 2009 4:32 AM
To: Jo-Ann Birch
Subject: Re: Missing Shoe

He is a sweet, sweet boy and you are great Moms. Thanks for the overnight.

Of course Anne loved you all. Me 2.

e

On 9/19/09 12:39 PM, "Jo-Ann Birch" <jbirch@email.com> wrote:

> Hi E,
>
> You were right about your shoe. He did hide it, because he didn't
> want you to leave.
>
> xo
>
> J

Soul Light

My father came to me in a meditation,
asking for my forgiveness.

My face knotted into folds of grief.
I told him I missed him.

Standing in his company again, I was
glad to be included in his justice.

He said he was a boob of a father.
I laughed out loud at his ability

to make the truth funny,
even from way over there.

Before returning to our ancestral
hoop, he told me he loves me.

He has changed in the eight years
since his passing, and I too.

I said I would forgive him,
but I didn't want him to go away.

At least with a grudge I'd had a connection,
even if it was the wrong kind.

So now I have set us both free.
Maybe I'll see him again, maybe not,

but it was the right thing to do,
something I'd learned from my father.

October

On our way to falling asleep last night,
my wife told me her mother bled that day
all over herself, the hospital bed, the floor.

She had received two pints of blood,
and because she has almost no platelets,
a pressure bandage stopped the bleeding.

And how her sister had to apply
a second bandage after she
got her mother home to bed.

I held my wife,
kissed her forehead,
rubbed her shoulders.

After awhile I said,
The Giants won, they're going to the World Series.
Good, she said without any hesitation.

Writing Group

beyond my knees, balancing the empty journal
beyond the coffee table and the orange dancing candle
beyond the beads hanging in the door
beyond the blue stained glass over the sink
beyond the window framed in lace
beyond the thick redwood holding the yellow feeder
beyond the weaving branches of the live oak tree
I saw a bird

Poetry

Poetry is the voice of kicking cosmos,
the crack through which all creation scrambles to be seen.

Poetry is the luxurious release of will,
traceable by a single set of fingerprints.

Poetry is the surest way to make a point,
enclosed in crescent moon quotation marks.

Poetry is the beaded mirror,
a made-up friend, forever faithful.

The Way of the World

Once there were two stooges who bumbled about,
walking into walls, talking nonsense,
trying to eat each other's limbs.

Because God wanted to see himself
in the world, he let the stooges
have babies, hoping for a miracle.

One, two, three girls were born
to the stooges, and the girls were
human and God was happy.

Having nowhere to go, the human
girls stayed with the stooges
for many, many years

where they learned to take only
what they needed and stay still
to avoid being noticed.

The stooges bumbled about, talking
nonsense, sitting on their heads,
trying to eat their limbs.

Then one night, when the girls had
learned enough about the world,
they left the stooges' hut, one by one.

Each learned to make food, have a home
of her own, keep company with other
humans, avoid the stooges.

One learned to paint, and God smiled.
Another led a social movement,
and God rejoiced in her following.

The third worked on ridding
herself of the menacing voices,
one word at a time.

ABOUT THE AUTHOR

Jo-Ann Birch grew up in Canada and emigrated to the U.S. in 1984. She began writing poetry while attending the University of California, Santa Cruz in the 1990's. Jo-Ann has been a selected reader for *In Celebration of the Muse*, an annual literary event featuring women writers of Santa Cruz County, and for *Poet/Speak*, a monthly venue featuring local poets. She has had her work published in *The Porter Gulch Review* anthology, the *Santa Cruz Sentinel* and *San Francisco Examiner* newspapers.

Jo-Ann lives in Santa Cruz, California with her partner and their son.

Made in the USA
Charleston, SC
15 January 2011